LADIES
OF
STRENGTH

Doris McKelvey is a retired elementary teacher.

Her assignment is to write easy to understand informational books for the Kingdom of God.

mckelvey.doris@yahoo.com

McKelvey & McKelvey Ministries

P. O. Box 106

Carthage, Texas 75633

Lady	Character Trait
Hannah	Promise Keeper
Rahab	Decision Maker
Deborah	Wise Leader
Jael	Problem Solver
Abigail	Courageous
Jochebed	Unselfish
Ruth	Virtuous
Tamar	Determined

Lady	Character Trait
Sarah	Patience
Priscilla	Teacher
Woman	Persistence
Dorcas	Helpful
Anna	Discernment
Mary	Listener
Woman	Focused
Mary	Mother

HANNAH

Promise Keeper   1 Samuel 1:1-28

There was a man with two wives. One was named Hannah.

The other wife had children but Hannah had none.

Because of this, Hannah suffered teasing and ridicule from the other wife, who had given the husband several children.

Each year the family went up to Shiloh to worship and sacrifice to the LORD.

The husband gave the other wife, sons, and daughters portions to be offered.

But to Hannah, he gave a double portion because he **loved** her.

One year, Hannah became so irritated with the other wife that she cried and would not eat.

"Hannah, why are you weeping? Why are you not eating? Why is thy heart grieved? Am not I better to thee than ten sons?" The husband asked.

He expected the consistent love and affection from him should be enough to ease her pain.

Afterwards, Hannah went to the temple to pray and cry unto the LORD.

Hannah made a vow. "Give me a man child, then I will give him unto the LORD all the days of his life."

As she prayed in her heart, the lips moved but she did not speak out loud.

Eli, the priest sat upon a seat by a post of the temple. He observed Hannah and thought that she was drunk. "How long will thy be drunk? Put away thy wine," he said.

Hannah answered and said, "I am a woman of sorrowful spirit: I have drunk neither wine nor strong drink, but I have poured out my soul before the LORD."

Then Eli the priest answered, "Go in peace: and the God of Israel grant thee thy petition that thou asked of him."

 Hannah was no longer sad when she left the temple.

———————

Over time, Hannah's prayer was answered. She conceived and gave birth to a son and named him Samuel.

When she had weaned him, she took him to the house of the LORD and left him with Eli, the priest.

Year after year, Hannah went with her husband to the temple to offer their yearly sacrifice. And each year she took Samuel a little coat that she had made for him. The LORD was with him.

Samuel grew up in the temple learning the duties of the priesthood.

It was there that Samuel heard the voice of the LORD calling him. (1 Samuel 3:1-21)

During his lifetime, Samuel served as a prophet, priest, and judge. (1 Samuel chapters 1-7)

REFLECTIONS

Hannah prayed unto the LORD for a miracle and her faithfulness was rewarded.

She remained true to her words. After she had gotten what she wanted from God, she did not fail to keep her promise.

God rewarded Hannah for her honor and sacrifice. She was blessed with three more sons and two daughters.

- God hears our prayers.
- Believe that our prayers are heard.
- Have faith.
- What I sacrifice for God will yield increase beyond measure.

Have you ever made promises to God? I have.

LORD, if you get me out of this, I will _____.

Does this sound familiar?

Can God trust me to keep my promise?

_____

_____

_____

_____

_____

Am I willing to give God what is HIS, even when I want to keep it for myself?

_____

_____

_____

_____

_____

When HE gives me what I want, is important that I keep my promise(s) to HIM? Explain.

_____

_____
_____
_____
_____
_____

What promise have I made to the LORD?

_____
_____
_____
_____
_____
_____
_____
_____
_____
_____

Study Scriptures

Psalm 66:18-20

If I regard iniquity in my heart, the Lord will not hear *me:*

But verily God hath heard *me*; he hath attended to the voice of *my* prayer.

Blessed be God, which hath not turned away my prayer, nor his mercy from me.

Luke 1:45

And blessed *is* she that believed for there shall be a performance of those things which were told her from the Lord.

Luke 6:38

Give, and it shall be given unto you; good measure, pressed down, and shaken together, and running over, shall men give into your bosom. For with the same measure that ye mete with it shall be measured to you again.

1 Timothy 2:8

I will therefore that men pray everywhere, lifting up holy hands, without wrath and doubting.

James 1:6-8

But let him ask in faith, nothing wavering. For he that waver is like a wave of the sea driven with the wind tossed.

For let not that man think that he shall receive any thing of the Lord.

A double minded man *is* unstable in all his ways.

Psalm 134:

Lift up your hands in the sanctuary, and bless the LORD.

Matthew 7:7-8

_____
_____
_____
_____
_____
_____
_____
_____
_____
_____

Luke 11:9-10

_____
_____
_____
_____
_____
_____
_____

RAHAB

Decision Maker   Joshua 2:1-24

After the death of Moses, the LORD spoke to Joshua to cross over Jordan onto the land promised to the children of Israel.

> Every place that the sole of your foot shall tread upon, that have I given unto you. (Joshua 1:3)

Joshua sent two men to search out the country saying, "Go view the land, even Jericho."

The two spies went and stopped at a harlot's house named Rahab.

When the king of Jericho heard of the two strangers, he sent a messenger to ask Rahab to reveal their identity.

Rahab decided to help Joshua's men. She lied and told the king's messengers that the two strangers had left.

"Pursue after them quickly and you will overtake them." She sent them on a false trail.

She had hidden Joshua's men on the rooftop of her house with the stalks of flax, a plant used for making linen.

After the king's men were gone, she went upon the roof to talk to the two spies.

Rahab confessed to Joshua's men that she had heard of their God. "He is God in heaven and on earth."

We have heard how the LORD dried up the waters of the Red Sea for them when they came out of Egypt.

She knew the Israelites had come to take over Jericho.

Rahab made a deal with the spies. She requested safety for her family. "Since I have showed you kindness, you will let my family live when you come to take this land."

"Our lives for your lives." The two men agreed.

She suggested that they hide in the mountains for three days until the king's men stop looking for them.

Rahab would bring her family into her house for safety. If she told the king about them, then the agreement would be broken.

Rahab let the two spies down with a scarlet cord through the window. Because her house was built on the wall of the city, the two spies escaped without harm.

She gathered her father, mother, brothers, sisters, and all that they had into her house. Then she placed the scarlet cord in the window where the spies were released.

———————

After three days the spies returned to Joshua.

When the Israelites captured Jericho, the house with the scarlet cord was not destroyed.

Rahab's household and family survived because of her declaration of faith in God and her willingness to help.

REFLECTIONS

God can and will use ordinary people to do extraordinary things!

God used Rahab, a prostitute, to bless the spies from the children of Israel.

The LORD looked at the heart of Rahab. HE did not judge her based on what she looked like or on her occupation.

Rahab's belief in what she had heard, prompted her to take action, and boldly accepted the God of Israel as her LORD.

Rahab is mentioned by name as a hero of faith in **Hebrews 11.**

- Faith without work is dead.
- Have faith in God.
- Man looks on the outward appearance, but the LORD looks on the heart.

My past mistakes will not cancel my future success. This is good news!

I have heard of miraculous things that the LORD has done for others that caused me to increase my faith.

What have I heard that gives me faith to believe?

_____

_____

_____

_____

_____

_____

_____

_____

_____

_____

_____

_____

_____

_____

Rahab was available to be used for the service of the LORD. She connected her belief with her actions.

How am I available to the service of the LORD?

_____

_____

_____

_____

_____

_____

_____

_____

_____

_____

_____

_____

_____

_____

Study Scriptures

Hebrews 11:31

By faith the harlot Rahab perished not with them that believed not, when she had received the spies with peace.

Hebrews 11:1

Now faith is the substance of things hoped for, the evidence of things not seen.

Acts 16:31

Believe on the Lord Jesus Christ, and thou shall be saved, and thy house.

James 2:25

Was not Rahab the harlot justified by works, when she had received the messengers, and had sent them out another way?

James 2:14-26

_____

_____

_____

_____

_____

_____

_____

_____

_____

_____

_____

_____

_____

_____

_____

_____

_____

_____

_____

_____

_____

DEBORAH

Wise Leader   Judges 4:1-24

Again, the children of Israel began to worship false gods and did evil in the sight of the LORD.

As punishment, the LORD delivered them into the hands of their enemy, king of Canaan.

The children of Israel cried unto the LORD for they had been oppressed for twenty years.

Deborah, a prophetess, judged Israel during this time. She dwelt under a palm tree.

The children of Israel went to her for judgement, direction, and guidance.

Deborah summoned Barak, a military leader, and said unto him, "Hath not the LORD God of Israel commanded, *saying,* Go and draw toward mount Tabor and take with thee ten thousand men?"

The LORD would lure Sisera, the captain of the king's army with his chariots, unto Barak.

And Barak said to Deborah, "If thou will go with me, then I will go: but if thou will not go with me, then I will not go."

Deborah agreed to go with him.

But because Barak decided to change the plan and include Deborah, he would not gain the honor from the victory.

Deborah prophesied that the LORD would deliver the captain of the enemy's army into the hands of a woman

REFLECTIONS

The people recognized that the LORD was with Deborah. She was a prophetess and the fifth judge of Israel.

After the victory, the people created a song of praise about Deborah and Barak.

- Deborah was a woman of wisdom.

- She knew that God would give them victory over the enemy.

The children of Israel came to Deborah for prayer and repentance.

As Christians, we all have gifts and talents to be used to uplift the kingdom of God.

I am grateful and thankful when others can experience the love of Jesus Christ through my words and actions.

What am I called to do?

_____

_____

_____

_____

_____

_____

_____

_____

_____

Study Scriptures

Proverbs 31:26

She opened her mouth with wisdom: and in her tongue is the law of kindness.

Proverbs 3:5-6

Trust in the LORD with all thine heart; and lean not unto thine own understanding.

In all thy ways acknowledge him, and he shall direct thy paths.

Psalm 37:4-5

Delight thyself also in the LORD; and he shall give thee the desires of thine heart.

Commit thy way unto the LORD; trust also in him; and he shall bring *it* to pass.

JAEL

Problem Solver   Judges 4:17-24

The captain of the Canaanite army, Sisera, climbed down off his chariot and fled away on feet during the battle with Barak and Deborah's warriors.

Barak pursued after the chariots and their army and the enemy fell upon the edge of the sword: and there was not a man left.

Sisera ran away to the tent of Jael. There was peace between the king of Canaan and her husband's people.

Jael went out to meet the runaway captain.

"Turn in to me, my lord; fear not," she said. The captain went into her tent and she hid him.

He asked for water to drink. She gave him some milk and covered him.

The captain asked her to stand guard in the door of the tent. If any man come to inquire, is there any man here? Thou shall say, no.

The captain fell fast asleep because he was weary and tired.

Jael took a nail of the tent and took a hammer in her hand and went softly unto him.

She smote the nail into his temples and fastened it into the ground. The captain died.

As Barak approached the tent, Jael went out to meet him. "Come, and I will show thee the man who thou seek," she said.

The children of Israel prospered and prevailed against Canaan. They sang a victory song of Deborah and Barak, and praised Jael for her actions.

REFLECTIONS

The captain accepted Jael's invitation to hide in the tent because he considered her husband's people a friend to the king.

This reminds me to check my acquaintances.

Can I accurately determine if a person is a friend or an enemy?

Who do I turn to in the time of trouble?

_____
_____
_____
_____
_____
_____
_____
_____
_____
_____
_____

- Jael made a decision to defeat the enemy.
- Deborah's prophecy came to pass. The captain was delivered into the hands of a woman.

Study Scriptures

Judges 5:24

Blessed above women shall Jael be, blessed shall she be above women in the tent.

Psalm 46:1

God is our refuge and strength, a very present help in trouble.

Psalm 34:4

I sought the LORD, and he heard me, and delivered me from all my fears.

Psalm 118:8

It is better to trust in the LORD than to put confidence in man.

ABIGAIL

Courageous   1 Samuel 25:2-42

Nabal was a wealthy man, but he was evil.

His wife, Abigail, was a woman of good understanding and very beautiful.

David sent ten men to Nabal for food and supplies for he heard that this man was prosperous in the business of sheep shearing.

The ten men were told to greet Nabal in the name of David. Speak peace to him, to his household, and unto all he has.

They were to tell Nabal that when his shepherds were with David's men, they were not hurt and none of the sheep were missing.

In return, David expected Nabal to give his men food and supplies since he had profited from shearing because of the protection of David's men.

Nabal answered and said, "Who is David? Shall I take my bread, and my water, and my meat and give it unto men, whom I know not?"

The ten men turned around and went back to David and reported what Nabal had said.

David was angry. "Put on your swords!"

He took about four hundred men with him to fight and kill Nabel and his household.

Meanwhile, one of Nabal's men went to Abigail to explain the situation.

> Behold, David sent messengers out of the wilderness to send greetings to our master, but he insulted them.

> David's men protected us and the sheep when we were in the fields.

> They were a wall unto us both by night and day all the while we were keeping the sheep," he explained.

> Now consider that David's army will surely attack our master and all of his household.

Abigail quickly ordered the servants to gather two hundred loaves, two bottles of wine, and five sheep ready dressed, five measures of parched corn, a hundred clusters of raisins, and two hundred cakes of figs. They loaded these things on donkeys.

She decided not tell her husband.

She hoped her actions would save all of them from death.

When Abigail saw David, she fell at his feet and bowed to the ground as a sign of respect and honor.

She begged David to disregard Nabel for he was foolish to reward good with evil.

> "Please accept these gifts of blessings for your men, said Abigail. I pray thee forgive me. I did not see the messengers that you sent.
>
> That this shall be no grief unto thee, nor offense of heart; neither shed blood or avenged thyself." She said.

David said to Abigail,

> "Blessed be the LORD God of Israel, which sent thee this day to meet me: And

blessed be thy advice, and blessed be thou, which has kept me from avenging myself with mine own hand."

David received all that she had brought him.

"Go in peace to thine house," he said.

Abigail returned home. Her husband had held a feast like a king. His heart was merry and he was drunk; therefore, she told him nothing about the meeting with David.

In the morning, when the wine was gone out of her husband, she told him the things that had happened.

His heart died within him and he became as a stone.

And it came to pass about ten days after, the LORD smote Nabal, and he died.

When David heard of Nabal's death, he was thankful that Abigail changed his mind about inflicting evil upon her husband.

David sent word to Abigail asking her to become his wife. She agreed.

REFLECTIONS

Abigail showed great strength and courage to approach David with food and supplies after her husband had refused to help him.

She decided to do the right thing at the risk of provoking her husband to anger.

Her actions changed David's mind and saved her household.

- Abigail took a risk. She did a responsible thing in an emergency situation.
- She acknowledged David and respected his authority of importance to Israel.

When am I courageous enough to do the right thing when others choose to do wrong?

_____

_____

_____

_____

_____

_____

_____

_____

_____

_____

_____

_____

_____

_____

_____

_____

_____

_____

Study Scriptures

Psalm 31:24

Be of good courage, and he shall strengthen your heart, all ye that hope in the LORD.

Proverbs 15:1

A soft answer turns away wrath: but grievous words stir up anger.

Proverbs 21:14

A gift in secret pacifies anger:

JOCHEBED

Unselfish   Exodus 2:1-10

Pharaoh commanded that every Hebrew son born shall be cast into the river to die.

_____

Jochebed had a son and hid him for three months.

When she could no longer hide him, she made a basket out of bulrush or papyrus and coated it with tar, slime, and pitch.

Then she placed the child in the basket and put it among the plants along the bank of the Nile River.

His sister stood at a distance to see and know what would happen to him.

Pharaoh's daughter went down to the river to wash herself. When she saw the ark, she sent her maid to fetch it.

When she opened it, she saw the child and the baby wept.

She had compassion on him and said,

> "This is one of the Hebrews' children.

Then the boy's sister said to Pharaoh's daughter,

> "Shall I go and call to thee a nurse of the Hebrew women, that she may nurse the child for thee?"

Pharaoh's daughter agreed.

The girl went to get the baby's mother, Jochebed.

Pharaoh's daughter said unto her,

> "Take this child away, and nurse it for me, and I will give thy wages. Jochebed took the child and nursed it.

The child grew and became Pharaoh's daughter's son.

She called his name Moses, "Because I drew him out of the water."

REFLECTIONS

- Jochebed protected her son from death.
- She gave him away so that he could live.
- Becoming the nurse allowed Jochebed to feed and care for the child she had birthed.
- God had a plan and a purpose for Moses.

As a Hebrew slave, his mother could not mentor Moses for the future that God had for him.

Pharaoh's daughter provided position in the palace where Moses received an education and preparation for his destiny.

Later in life, when Moses learned that he was Hebrew, he did not hate his mother for the choice she made to give him a better life.

- Jochebed is listed as one of the heroes of faith in **Hebrews** chapter 11.

What am I hiding? Is it for my good? Or NOT?

_____

_____

_____

_____

_____

_____

_____

_____

_____

_____

_____

_____

_____

_____

_____

_____

_____

_____

_____

_____

_____

Study Scriptures

Hebrews 11:23

By faith Moses, when he was born, was hid three months of his parents because they saw he was a proper child; and they were not afraid of the king's commandment.

Acts 7:20-23

In which time Moses was born, and was exceeding fair, and nourished up in his father's house for three months.

And when he was cast out, Pharaoh's daughter took him up, and nourished him for her own son.

And Moses was learned in all the wisdom of the Egyptians, and was mighty in words and in deeds.

RUTH

Virtuous   Ruth 1 – 4

After her husband died, Ruth did not return to her mother's house. She decided to stay with Naomi, her mother-in-law.

Ruth turned away from her people and their pagan heritage and followed Naomi back to Bethlehem.

- Ruth accepted the LORD as her God.

The two women arrived in Bethlehem during the barley harvest.

Ruth was given permission to glean in the field of Boaz, a wealthy relative of Naomi's deceased husband.

The fatherless and widows were allowed to gather the grain left behind by the reapers. This was a system for helping those in need.

Boaz instructed his men to not harm Ruth and to leave extra in the fields for her to gather.

At the end of the harvest, Naomi wanted to secure a home for Ruth since she was displaced in a foreign land without proper protection in their society.

- Naomi mentored Ruth.

After following their routines and traditions, Boaz gained the right to marry Ruth. They had a son named Obed.

REFLECTIONS

Ruth's faithfulness to Naomi led to a new life.

Her status changed from poverty with no husband to wealthy and married.

Ruth was a stranger in the field but ended up owning the fields as Boaz's wife.

- God opened doors for Ruth.
- Let go of the past. Look to the future.
- Have moral excellence.

Naomi was a wise and devoted advisor to Ruth.

**Who has given me good advice? Did I listen?
What was the outcome?**

_____

_____

_____

_____

_____

_____

_____

_____

_____

_____

_____

_____

_____

_____

_____

_____

_____

_____

_____

Study Scriptures

Proverbs 12:4

A virtuous woman is a crown to her husband.

Matthew 1:5-6a

Boaz begat Obed of Ruth: and Obed begat Jesse: And Jesse begat David the king:

Psalm 62:8

Trust in him at all times; pour out your heart before him: God is a refuge.

Psalm 37:3

Trust in the LORD, and do good; so shalt thou dwell in the land, and verily thou shalt be fed.

Ruth 3:11

_____
_____
_____
_____
_____

Ruth 1:16

_____
_____
_____
_____

Proverbs 31:10

_____
_____
_____
_____
_____

TAMAR

Determined Genesis 38:6-30

Judah was one of the twelve sons of Jacob. It was he that begged his brothers not to kill Joseph, but to sell their youngest brother to merchants. (Genesis 37:26-28)

Afterwards, Judah left home and went to live in another place. He married a Canaanite woman and they had three sons.

Tamar was the wife of Judah's firstborn son, Er. He was wicked in the sight of the LORD, and the LORD slew him.

Judah told Onan, the next son, "Go in unto thy brother's wife, marry her, and raise up the seed."

In their law, when a married man died without an heir, his next in line eligible brother was to marry the widow in order to produce an heir who would receive his brother's inheritance and carry on his name.

Onan knew that the offspring would not be as his child. So, he went in to Tamar, but spilled the semen on the ground so that she would not become pregnant.

This thing that he did displeased the LORD: and Onan died.

Then Judah said to Tamar, his daughter-in-law, "Remain a widow at thy father's house until Shelah, my third, is old enough to marry."

Tamar went and lived in her father's house and waited for the third son to come of age.

———————————

Judah did not follow through with his promise.

When Shelah, the third son, became grown, he was not given unto marriage to Tamar.

Judah's wife died. After his period of mourning was over, Judah went to sheer sheep with his friends.

When Tamar heard about this, she took off her widow's garments and covered her face with a veil. She wrapped herself and went to sit in an open place.

When Judah saw the woman, he thought her to be a prostitute and propositioned her. He did not know that the woman was Tamar.

"Let me come in unto thee." Judah said.

"What will thou give me that thou may come in unto me?" She asked.

He said, "I will give a baby goat from the flock."

She said, "Will thou give me a pledge, till thou send it?"

"What pledge shall I give thee?" Judah asked.

She said, "Thy signet, and thy bracelets, and thy staff that is in thine hand."

And he gave it to her and went in unto her, and she conceived by him.

Tamar arose and went away. She took off the veil and put on her garments of widowhood.

Later, Judah sent the baby goat by his friend to receive his pledge from the woman, but he found her not. He asked the men of the place, "Where is the harlot?"

They replied, "There is not prostitute in this place."

The man returned to Judah. He reported that he could not find the woman and that the men said, "There was no harlot in this place."

About three months later, it was told to Judah that his daughter-in-law, Tamar, is with child by whoredom.

Judah said, bring her forth and let her be burnt.

When Tamar was brought forth, she sent to her father-in-law saying, "By the man, who own these, am I with child: the signet, the bracelets, and staff, who are these?"

Judah acknowledged them and said, "She has been more *righteous* than I: because I gave her **not** to Shelah, my son."

Tamar had twin sons. Judah's lineage would continue. Judah and Tamar became ancestors of Jesus through their son, Perez.

REFLECTIONS

Because Judah withheld his third son from marrying Tamar, she made a drastic decision to take matters into her own hands.

Judah failed to fulfill his responsibilities and obligations as father and father-in-law.

Tamar decided to fight back. She did not want the enemy to steal her purpose in life.

Her determination changed their conversations from thinking she was the whorish widow to calling her a *righteous woman.*

- Judah judged Tamar as **"righteous."**

- The law stated in Deuteronomy 25:5-6 does not apply today.

What drastic decision(s) will I make to serve God?

_____

_____

_____

_____

_____

_____

_____

_____

_____

What am I determined to do?

_____

_____

_____

_____

It is human nature that allows us to see the wrong-doings of others but we are blind to our sins.

- According to the Bible, we are all sinners.
- Jesus Christ died for our sins.

Study Scriptures

Romans 3:23-24

For all have sinned, and come short of the glory of God.

Being justified freely by his grace through the redemption that is in Christ Jesus.

Romans 8:28

And we know that all things work together for good to them that love God, to them who are the called according to *his* purpose.

Matthew 1:3 (NIV)

Judah, the father of Perez and Zerah, whose mother was Tamar.

- A record of the genealogy of Jesus Christ includes Judah and Tamar.

Luke 6:41-42

_____

_____

_____

_____

_____

_____

_____

_____

_____

_____

_____

_____

Romans 5:19

_____

_____

_____

_____

_____

_____

1 John 1:8-10

_____

_____

_____

_____

_____

_____

_____

_____

_____

_____

_____

_____

SARAH

Patience   Genesis 17:16-22

God promised Abraham that he and his wife, Sarah, would have a son. She shall be a *mother* of nations.

Abraham laughed in his heart. Shall a *child* be born unto him at a hundred years old and his wife at ninety years of age?

God said, **"Sarah thy wife shall bear thee a son indeed: and thou shalt call his name Isaac: and I will establish my covenant with him for an everlasting covenant, *and* with his seed after him."**

Sarah shall bear a son unto Abraham at this set time next year.

_____ Genesis 18:1-15 _____

The LORD said to Abraham, **"Sarah thy wife shall have a son."**

Sarah laughed within herself. She doubted that this could happen because of her age.

- **Is any thing too hard for the LORD?**

At the time appointed I will return unto thee, according to the time of life, and Sarah shall have a son.

_____ Genesis 21:1-8 _____

The LORD did for Sarah as HE had promised.

Sarah conceived and bore Abraham a son in his old age, at the set time of which God had spoken to him.

Abraham was a hundred years old when his son Isaac was born unto him.

Sarah said,

> "God has made me to laugh, so that all that hear will laugh with me. Who would have said unto Abraham that Sarah

should have given children suck? For I have born him a son in his old age."

REFLECTIONS

All the evidence supported that it would be unlikely for Abraham and Sarah to have a child at their old ages.

- It is not uncommon to doubt what seems impossible.
- God keeps his promises! Hallelujah!

How long am I willing to wait for God's promise to be fulfilled?

_____

_____

_____

_____

_____

When have I not waited for God to provide the answer to my situation? How did I try to fix it?

_____

_____

_____

_____

_____

_____

_____

_____

_____

_____

_____

_____

_____

_____

_____

_____

_____

_____

Study Scriptures

Roman 9:9

For this is the word of promise, AT THIS TIME WILL I COME, AND SARAH SHALL HAVE A SON.

Galatians 4:28

Now we, brethren, as Isaac was, are the children of promise.

Luke 1:37

For with God nothing shall be impossible.

Hebrews 11:11

Through faith also Sarah herself received strength to conceive seed, and was delivered of a child when she was past age, because she judged him faithful who had promised.

Psalm 27:14

Wait on the LORD: be of good courage, and he shall strengthen thine heart; wait, I say, on the LORD.

Isaiah 40:31

But they that wait upon the LORD shall renew their strength; they shall mount up with wings as eagles; they shall run, and not be weary; and they shall walk, and not faint.

Romans 4:16-25

_____

_____

_____

_____

_____

_____

_____

_____

_____

PRISCILLA

Teacher   Acts 18:24-26

After the emperor commanded all Jews to depart from Rome, Paul sailed to Corinth.

There he met Jewish Christians Aquila and his wife Priscila.

They traveled with Paul to Ephesus when he went into the synagogue to reason with the Jews.

———————

A certain Jew, named Apollos, came to Ephesus. He was a learned man with a thorough knowledge of the scriptures.

This man was instructed in the way of the Lord: and being fervent (passionate and intense) in the spirit, he spoke and taught diligently the things of the Lord.

He taught about Jesus accurately, but knew only about the baptism of John.

When Aquila and Priscilla heard Apollos speak boldly in the synagogue, they invited him to their house and instructed him more thoroughly in the Christian faith.

REFLECTIONS

Priscilla and her husband were followers of Jesus.

They had traveled with Paul at least on one occasion.

- Priscilla was devoted to the Christian cause.
- She taught Christianity in their home with her husband.

Am I willing to teach others about Jesus?

Who? When? Where?

_____

_____

_____

_____

_____

_____

_____

_____

_____

_____

_____

_____

_____

_____

_____

_____

_____

_____

_____

_____

_____

Study Scriptures

Romans 16:3

Greet Priscilla and Aquila, my helpers in Christ Jesus.

Isaiah 28:9

Whom shall he teach knowledge? And whom shall he make to understand doctrine?

Ephesians 4:11

_____

_____

_____

_____

Jeremiah 9:20

_____

_____

WOMAN

WITH THE

ISSUE

OF

BLOOD

Persistence   Mark 5:25-34

A certain woman had an issue of blood for twelve years.

She had suffered many things of many physicians, and had spent all that she had.

Her condition had not improved but rather grew worse.

When she had heard of Jesus, she pressed behind him and touched his garment.

For she said, "If I may touch but his clothes, I shall be whole."

The fountain of her blood was dried up; and she felt in *her* body that she was healed.

Immediately Jesus knew that the virtue had gone out of him, and turned about to the crowd and said, **"Who touched my clothes?"**

He looked around to see who had done this thing.

But the woman fearing and trembling, knowing what was done in her, came and fell down before him, and told him all the truth.

And he said unto her, **"Daughter, thy faith hath made thee whole; go in peace, and be whole of thy plague."**

REFLECTIONS

- The woman was healed of her affliction.
- In spite of her physical difficulty, the woman pressed through the crowd.
- She had strong faith.

What are my issues? (physical, medical, financial, emotional)

_____

_____

_____

_____

_____

Study Scriptures

Psalm 51:1-2

Have mercy upon me, O God, according to thy lovingkindness: according unto the multitude of thy tender mercies blot not my transgression.

Wash me thoroughly from mine iniquity, and cleanse me from my sin.

Philippians 3:14

I press toward the mark for the prize of the high calling of God in Christ Jesus.

Luke 9:43-48

_____

_____

_____

_____

_____

DORCAS

Helper   Acts 9:36-42

Dorcas was a Christian woman known for her work to help the needy.

She became sick and died. They washed her body and laid her in an upper chamber.

When they heard that Peter was in the nearby town, two men were sent with a message to ask him to come to them.

When Peter arrived, they brought him to the upper chamber.

All the widows stood by him weeping and showing the coats and clothes which Dorcas made for the poor.

Peter put everyone out of the room. He kneeled down, prayed, and said, "arise."

Dorcas opened her eyes. When she saw Peter, she sat up.

He gave her his hand and lifted her up. Peter called the saints and widows and presented Dorcas alive.

This news spread all through the city.

Many believed in the Lord upon seeing Dorcas raised from the dead.

REFLECTIONS

Dorcas did many good works of mercy as she helped the poor.

What good deeds am I doing for the Kingdom of God?

_____

_____

_____

_____

_____

_____

_____

How am I letting my light shine so that others may believe in Jesus Christ?

_____

_____

_____

_____

_____

_____

_____

Study Scriptures

Psalm 29:4

The voice of the LORD is powerful;

Titus 3:8

_____

_____

_____

_____

ANNA

Discernment   Luke 2:36-38

Anna was a prophetess. She could foretell future events through divine inspiration.

She was a widow and departed not from the temple, but served God with fasting and prayers night and day.

Anna was at the temple in Jerusalem when Mary and Joseph brought Jesus to be dedicated.

Anna perceived Jesus as the Messiah, the King of the Jews.

REFLECTIONS

- Fast and Pray.
- Anticipate. Distinguish. Understand.

It is important to know the word of God. This will allow me to recognize when HE speaks to me and guide me to make decisions that will please HIM.

As Christians, we accept Jesus as our spiritual deliverer.

HE is the one anointed by God and empowered with God's spirit to deliver HIS people and establish HIS kingdom.

Jesus sets us free from sin and spiritual death.

When have I had a strong understanding or judgement about something?

_____

_____

_____

_____

_____

What am I willing to avoid or go without for a period of time (fasting)? Why?

_____

_____

_____

_____

Study Scriptures

1 Timothy 5:5

Now she that is a widow indeed, and desolate, trust in God, and continue in supplications and prayers night and day.

Matthew 6: 16-18 (Fasting)

_____

_____

_____

_____

_____

_____

Matthew 6:9-13   and   Luke 11:1-4 (Prayer)

_____

_____

_____

_____

MARY
AND
MARTHA

Listener   Luke 10:38-42

Mary and Martha were sisters. Jesus and the disciples visited their house after their brother Lazarus was raised from the dead.

Mary sat at Jesus' feet and listened to HIS teaching while Martha worked in the kitchen preparing for the meal.

Martha went to Jesus saying, "Lord, do you care not that my sister left me to serve alone? Bid her to help me."

Jesus answered and said unto her,

Martha, Martha, thou art careful and troubled about many things.

But one thing is needful: and Mary has chosen that good part, which shall not be taken away from her."

REFLECTIONS

Both sisters loved Jesus; however, each had different behaviors on this day.

Martha was focused on feeding the body for physical need and nourishment.

Mary listened attentively to the teaching by Jesus for the feeding of the mind and soul.

- Mary was not distracted. She was alert.

How may I please the Lord without distractions?

_____

_____

_____

_____

_____

_____

_____

_____

_____

Study Scriptures

John 11:5

Now Jesus loved Martha, and her sister, and their brother Lazarus.

John 11:43-44

_____

_____

_____

John 12:1-11

_____

_____

_____

_____

_____

_____

_____

_____

A
WOMAN

Focused　　Luke 7:36-39

One of the Jewish leaders invited Jesus to his house to eat.

A woman in the city, which was a sinner, went to the house when she heard Jesus was there.

She stood at HIS feet weeping. She washed Jesus' feet with her tears and wiped them with her hair.

She kissed HIS feet and anointed them with a perfumed ointment in an alabaster box.

When the Jewish leader saw this, he spoke within himself saying,

> "This man, if he were a prophet, would have known who and what manner of woman this is that touched him, for she is a sinner."

Then Jesus taught the parable of the two debtors. HE turned to the woman and said unto the Simon,

> **"See this woman? I entered into thine house, thou gave me no water for my feet, but she washed my feet with tears and wiped them with the hairs on her head.**
>
> **Thou gave me no kiss, but this woman has not ceased to kiss my feet.**
>
> **My head with oil thou did not anoint; but this woman anointed my feet with her ointment.**
>
> **Wherefore I say unto thee, her sins which are many, are forgiven; for she loved much: but to whom little is forgiven, the same love little."**

Those that sat with him began to say within themselves, who is this that forgives sins also?

Jesus said to the woman,

"Thy faith has saved thee; go in peace."

REFLECTIONS

- This woman was a lady of strength.
- She was focused on Jesus.

I can only imagine the courage, boldness, and power it took for her to enter this house.

Since she was a known sinner, she probably expected a certain level of intensity in the room.

Some might have pointed fingers, called her names, or whispered gossip.

Yet, this woman did not allow others to hinder her plan. She poured the perfumed ointment as praise and worship to Jesus.

How am I focused on Jesus?

_____

_____

_____

_____

_____

_____

What have I presented to Jesus as praise and worship?

_____

_____

_____

_____

_____

_____

- Listen to the song, "The Alabaster Box" by Ce Ce Winans.

Study Scriptures

Matthew 6:14-15

For if ye forgive men their trespasses, your heavenly Father will also forgive you:

But if ye forgive not men their trespasses; neither will your Father forgive your trespasses.

Ephesians 4:32

Be ye kind one to another, tenderhearted, forgiving one another, even as God for Christ's sake has forgiven you.

Psalm 32:1-5

_____

_____

_____

_____

_____

_____

MARY

MOTHER
OF
JESUS

Mother   Luke 1:26-38

The angel Gabriel was sent from God into a city of Galilee, named Nazareth.

A virgin was betrothed to a man whose name was Joseph, of the house of David. The virgin's name was Mary.

The angel said to her,

> *"Hail, thou that are highly favored, the Lord is with thee: blessed are thou among women.*
>
> *Fear not Mary; for thou have found favor with God.*
>
> *Behold, thy shall conceive in thy womb, and bring forth a son, and shall call his name JESUS.*
>
> *He shall be great, and shall be called the Son of the Highest, and the Lord God shall give unto him the throne of his father, David:*

He shall reign over the house of Jacob for ever and of his kingdom there shall be no end."

Then said Mary unto the angel, "How shall this be, seeing I know not a man?"

The angel answered and said unto her,

"The Holy Ghost shall come upon thee and the power of the Highest shall overshadow thee: also, that holy thing which shall be born of thee shall be called the Son of God."

Mary said, "Behold the handmaid of the Lord: be it unto me according to thy word."

Then, the angel departed from her.

_____ Luke 2:1-7 _____

Joseph went from Galilee, out of the city of David, which is called Bethlehem: (because he was of the house and lineage of David).

His wife, Mary, was great with child. She brought forth her firstborn son, and wrapped him in swaddling clothes, and laid him in a manger; because there was no room for them in the inn.

_____ John 19:25-27 _____

Mary was there with her son, Jesus, while he was being crucified on the cross.

When Jesus saw his mother and the disciple standing by, whom he loved, he said unto his mother, *"Woman, behold thy son!"*

Then said he to the disciple, *"Behold thy mother!"*

Jesus made arrangements for his mother to be take care of after his death.

And from that hour the beloved disciple took Mary into his own home.

Jesus was received up into heaven and sat on the right hand of God.

In the upper room, the disciples and the women, continued with one accord in prayer.

Mary, the mother of Jesus, was with them.

REFLECTIONS

It takes a lady of strength to witness the crucifixion of her child on the cross.

She endured the agony as her son was nailed to the cross, beaten, made to wear a crown of thorns, given vinegar for water, and pierced in the side.

- Mary did not leave her son.
- She was faithful to her belief that Jesus was the Son of God.

- She was in the upper room with the disciples for the coming of the Holy Spirit.

As a mother, how do I support my child(ren)?

_____
_____
_____
_____
_____
_____
_____
_____
_____
_____
_____
_____
_____
_____
_____
_____
_____
_____

Study Scriptures

Luke 1:37

For with God nothing shall be impossible.

Luke 2:25-35

_____

_____

_____

_____

_____

_____

John 2:5

Mary told the servants to do whatsoever her son tells them. Jesus turned the water into wine because his mother asked.

Luke 1:48

All generations shall call Mary blessed.

Acknowledgements

The title of this book, **Ladies of Strength**, was inspired by my membership in a social club for women.

Lady Bernice

Lady Bert

Lady Beverly

Lady Clovis

Lady Cynthia

Lady Faye

Lady Gloria

Lady Gracie

Lady Judy

Lady Linda

Lady Peggy

Lady Sedonia

- *In Memory of Lady Glenda*

I am forever grateful to my mama, Everlean, as my role model and the ultimate example of a strong woman. **I love you!**

A big shout out to my aunts, sisters, cousins, and nieces!

Thank you to all the ladies who have inspired me professionally and spiritually!

Proverbs 31:30

> **A woman that fears the LORD, she shall be praised.**

Other Books by Doris McKelvey

Informational

- Secret Things
- Text Messages from God
- A Relationship with Jesus
- The Decision: Life or Death

Christian Fiction

- Distractions

Books are available on **www.amazon.com** and other online book retailers.

Made in the USA
Middletown, DE
18 September 2022